INCREDIBLY DISGUSTING FOOD™

CARBONATED BEVERAGES

THE INCREDIBLY DISGUSTING STORY

Adam•Furgang

rosen publishing's
rosen central

New York

To Ben

Published in 2011 by The Rosen Publishing Group, Inc.
29 East 21st Street, New York, NY 10010

Copyright © 2011 by The Rosen Publishing Group, Inc.

First Edition

Library of Congress Cataloging-in-Publication Data

Furgang, Adam.
Carbonated beverages: the incredibly disgusting story / Adam Furgang.
    p. cm.—(Incredibly disgusting food)
Includes bibliographical references and index.
ISBN 978-1-4488-1266-0 (library binding)
ISBN 978-1-4488-2282-9 (pbk.)
ISBN 978-1-4488-2286-7 (6-pack)
1. Carbonated beverages—Health aspects—Juvenile literature. I. Title.
TP630.F87 2011
613.2—dc22

2010023227

Manufactured in the United States of America

CPSIA Compliance Information: Batch #W11YA: For further information, contact Rosen Publishing, New York, New York, at 1-800-237-9932.

CONTENTS

INTRODUCTION

There's that distinctive, unmistakable sound. The fizzing, cracking, refreshing sound of a soda can or bottle top popping open, releasing a frenzy of tiny, misty bubbles into the air. Is this a sound that makes you long for a refreshing pop?

Whether you call them soft drinks, soda pop, or just plain soda, carbonated beverages have been growing in popularity as a favorite American beverage since the 1800s. In fact, our love of carbonated soft drinks has been growing at an ever increasing rate over the past generation. Since 1978, the consumption of carbonated beverages has tripled for males between the ages of twelve and twenty-nine. It has doubled for females in the same age group. According to the National Soft Drink Association, the average person now consumes six hundred sodas per year, each at about 12 ounces (0.35 liters) per bottle. Males ages twelve to twenty-nine consume an average of 160 gallons (606 l) per year—almost 2 quarts (1.9 l) per day! That's a lot of soda.

It's no wonder why these drinks are so popular. We find these bubbly treats in vending machines, at parties, in restaurants, at schools, at sporting events, and taking up entire aisles at the grocery store. In the United States, carbonated beverages are often less expensive than other drinks, such as juices and sometimes even bottled water. We buy them in large containers, half a gallon (2 l) at a time, or we buy individual servings in packs of six or even by the case.

But what are these drinks made of? What are the ingredients, and how healthy or unhealthy are they? The short answer is that carbonated soft drinks do not contain anything that is very good for us. In fact, soft drinks are one of the major culprits in the obesity epidemic in the United States. A long list of chemicals, additives, and unhealthy sugar substitutes fill each can and bottle. At current levels of consumption among North American children, calories from soft drinks contribute up to 10 percent of their total daily intake of calories. Unfortunately, almost no nutritional value goes along with these calories.

Obesity is just the beginning. In addition, tooth decay, bad breath, hyper-activity, depression, gallstones, diabetes, high blood pressure, heart disease, stroke, cancer, and premature death are all possible consequences of drinking carbonated beverages in excess.

Soft drink serving sizes are increasing, intake is skyrocketing, and disease and illness are spreading. For these reasons, it has become of urgent impor-tance to learn about what kinds of ingredients actually go into carbonated beverages and what they can do to the human body. You may find that some incredibly disgusting things have made their way into your diet—and your body—without you even realizing it.

1

THAT'S WHY IT'S CALLED JUNK FOOD

Did you know that soft drinks used to be associated with health and well-being? From their first appearance in the 1600s and into the twentieth century, they were often marketed and consumed as medicinal "tonics."

Today, however, soft drinks have anything but a good reputation. Instead of being associated with health as they once were, they are now considered one of the worst junk foods that can be consumed. What happened to change perceptions about carbonated beverages? Changes to soda ingredients account for most of the negative health effects of carbonated beverages and the public's changing attitudes toward them.

The Incredibly Disgusting Ingredients

Carbonated beverages may seem like simple liquids. Yet they contain dozens of ingredients, including high fructose corn syrup, various sugars and sweeteners, caramel color, phosphoric acid, caffeine, and natural flavors (which are not as natural as you might suspect). Because of the high calorie count and sugar/sweetener content, many doctors, nutritionists, and health care workers have begun to refer to soft drinks as "liquid candy." Most of the individual ingredients in the average can of soda are unnatural, unhealthy, and unappetizing.

The ingredients contained in food and beverage products are always listed on product labels in descending order of quantity. So the first ingredient on the list is always the main or most plentiful ingredient in the food or drink. With carbonated beverages, water is the first ingredient and will therefore be at the top of the list. So far so good. Water is healthy, and humans need it to stay hydrated and survive. Yet the trouble starts with the very next ingredient on the list. Typically, right after water, some form of sweetener is listed. This is usually high fructose corn syrup, table sugar, or fruit juice sugar concentrates.

This vintage advertisement for Coca-Cola promotes the drink as a healthy tonic that relieves mental and physical exhaustion.

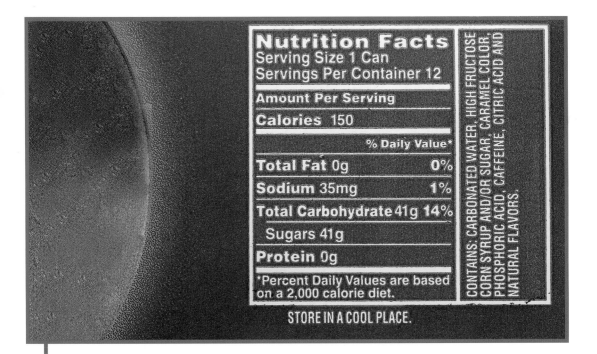

Nutrition Facts
Serving Size 1 Can
Servings Per Container 12

Amount Per Serving

Calories 150

% Daily Value*

Total Fat 0g   0%

Sodium 35mg   1%

Total Carbohydrate 41g 14%

  Sugars 41g

Protein 0g

*Percent Daily Values are based on a 2,000 calorie diet.

CONTAINS: CARBONATED WATER, HIGH FRUCTOSE CORN SYRUP AND/OR SUGAR, CARAMEL COLOR, PHOSPHORIC ACID, CAFFEINE, CITRIC ACID AND NATURAL FLAVORS.

STORE IN A COOL PLACE.

Nutrition labels show that sodas are high in calories and filled with unhealthy, unnatural ingredients.

High Fructose Corn Syrup

High fructose corn syrup (HFCS) is an artificial sweetener made from corn. This corn has often been genetically modified to resist the effects of poisonous pesticides. The syrup's widespread use in the United States did not begin until the 1970s, and obesity trends have continued to rise steadily ever since.

In North America today, HFCS accounts for about half of all added sugars in our diet. It has been reported that average consumption of HFCS is an alarming 73.5 pounds (33.3 kilograms) per person per year. Between 1970—when the ultrasweet syrup was first added to the North American diet—and 2000, adult obesity rates in the United States more than doubled from 15 percent to 30 percent. This means that by the beginning of the twenty-first century, almost one out of three American adults was obese. Today, about 17 percent of U.S. children between the ages of two and nineteen are considered obese.

Currently, a debate rages over whether or not high fructose corn syrup is getting a bad rap. Corn industry spokespeople and some food manufacturers dispute the link between the sweetener's increasing presence in our diet and rising rates of obesity. The corn industry even claims that HFCS is a natural—and therefore healthy—product because it comes from corn. Nutritionists, doctors, and other health groups counter that HFCS is a sugar substitute that is manufactured using chemicals, enzymes, and caustic (corrosive) soda. These harsh chemicals help change starch that is extracted from the corn into sweet and sugary fructose or glucose. Trace amounts of the highly toxic element mercury have even been found in HFCS as a result of some of these chemical processes.

Caramel Color

Another ingredient usually found right below high fructose corn syrup is caramel color. Like HFCS, caramel color is frequently made from corn. To give carbonated cola beverages their distinctly brown color, sugars and carbohydrates such as HFCS and other syrups are carefully burned with the addition of salts and acids. This process results in a mixture that smells like burned sugar. This caramelized substance gives color and flavor to many carbonated beverages like cola, root beer, and cream soda. As an ingredient, it is simply just another form of sugar.

Phosphoric Acid

Phosphoric acid is often the next item on a carbonated beverage's ingredient list. Phosphorus, the source mineral for phosphoric acid, is mined from rocks in the earth. After going through various chemical processes, the phosphorus is converted into phosphoric acid. This acid is quite common and powerful. It is used to make baking soda and can even be used for rust removal.

As with high fructose corn syrup, there is a lively debate surrounding phosphoric acid and its effects on the human body. Tooth decay and a higher instance of broken bones has been observed among carbonated soda drinkers. While phosphorus itself is an important part of our bones, a poor phosphorus-calcium ratio may lead to bone loss. The phosphoric acid in sodas may or may not be to blame for bone loss and weakening in soft drink consumers. Nevertheless, many studies point to the fact that by drinking more carbonated beverages, kids are getting too much phosphoric acid and far too little calcium. This is because they are drinking less milk in favor of carbonated beverages. Indeed, some children have no milk at all in their diet.

"Natural Flavors"

So-called "natural flavors" are another ingredient commonly found in many carbonated beverages. The term "natural flavors" is vague and misleading. The Food and Drug Administration (FDA) requires that an ingredient identified as a "natural flavor" must come from a natural source, such as chicken, beef, seafood, fruits, vegetables, tree bark, plant roots, or plant material.

Caffeinated beverages can give the consumer a quick energy fix, but then an energy "crash" can follow just as quickly.

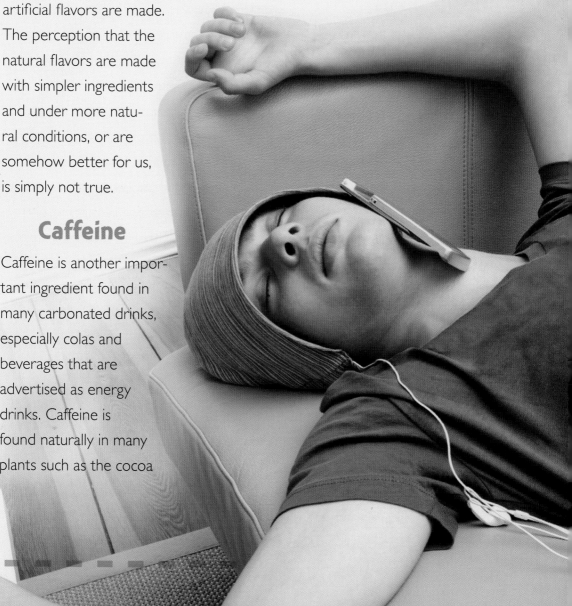

Often, however, flavors labeled as "natural" are actually created under controlled conditions with the addition of chemicals to the natural source. Consumers generally prefer the term "natural," but most of these flavors are actually produced chemically and in the same factories in which artificial flavors are made. The perception that the natural flavors are made with simpler ingredients and under more natural conditions, or are somehow better for us, is simply not true.

Caffeine

Caffeine is another important ingredient found in many carbonated drinks, especially colas and beverages that are advertised as energy drinks. Caffeine is found naturally in many plants such as the cocoa tree, from which cocoa and chocolate are derived. Caffeine also occurs naturally in coffee beans and tea leaves.

Pure caffeine is a stimulant that increases the body's heart rate, blood pressure, and other metabolic functions. When people drink beverages with caffeine in them, they become stimulated and have more energy. While this may give them an initial boost, there is an inevitable energy crash soon after.

Medical studies have now concluded that caffeine addiction is real. Many people become dependent on caffeinated beverages to wake themselves up, get going in the morning, and stay awake and energized throughout the day and into the evening. When someone who regularly consumes a lot of caffeine is forced to do without it for a day—or even several hours—he or she will frequently experience headaches, fatigue, drowsiness, depression, nausea, and concentration problems. These are caffeine withdrawal symptoms, and they are similar in kind and intensity to those of stronger illegal drugs.

Artificial Flavors and Colors

Even when they are decaffeinated, the wide variety of carbonated beverages on the market today feature many other harmful ingredients. These include natural sugars, artificial sweeteners, artificial and natural colors, and more. Many carbonated beverages, such as orange or grape soft drinks, contain odd-sounding coloring ingredients like red 48, blue 1, yellow 6, red 40, and more. The chemical benzene, a flammable oil, is used as the raw material for many food dyes.

Most carbonated beverages are artificially flavored and colored so that consumers associate them with the natural fruit that the sodas are imitating or approximating. Grape or orange soda may contain no actual grape or orange juice. Yet it is flavored, colored, and labeled in such a way as to create the convincing illusion that it is derived from a natural fruit source.

While the ingredients in carbonated beverages would not be harmful when consumed infrequently and in small amounts, today they are being consumed in great quantities every day. As a result, the health of North Americans is suffering greatly. The simple act of drinking too many sugary carbonated beverages too often is resulting in serious health problems for people. Health costs in the United States associated with obesity are now estimated at around $147 billion a year. This represents 10 percent of all annual medical spending.

MYTHS AND FACTS

Myth: Soda, even in small quantities, is bad for you.
Fact: If consumed only on special occasions and within an otherwise balanced diet, there is no harm in enjoying a soda once in a while.

Myth: The acid in carbonated beverages is so strong and caustic that an iron nail will dissolve in cola in a few hours.
Fact: Although this is not true, cola will still erode enamel and rot teeth more quickly and cause more tooth decay than most other drinks.

Myth: Real juice is better for you than soda.
Fact: Fruit juices such as apple, orange, and grape juice still contain high quantities of sugar and can add excess weight and pounds to your body. The best beverage choice, other than water and milk, is fresh-squeezed juice with no additives.

2

THE SHORT-TERM EFFECTS

Whenever we put a can or bottle to our lips, we rarely know what we are really drinking and what ingredients we are ingesting. Processed and unnatural ingredients affecting the health of the nation have crept into our carbonated beverages over the last few decades.

For starters, a single 12-ounce (340 grams) can of soda contains the equivalent of about 13 tablespoons (192 milliliters) of sugar. No one would think to mix all of that sugar into a glass of water and drink it. Yet each time we drink a sweetened carbonated beverage, that is exactly what we are doing. All the excess sugars and sweeteners, natural or human-made, are a shock to our systems. Our bodies are unable to process all this sugar. As a result, North Americans are developing a long list of diseases, some of them potentially fatal, at a younger and younger age.

Many of the ailments associated with poor dietary habits that used to be seen in adults in their fifties—such as diabetes, heart disease, and bone and joint problems—are now being seen in children as young as nine. So what used to be considered the long-term effects of a poor diet are now increasingly seen as short-term effects. The unhealthy foods and drinks that North Americans are consuming are taking the place of the nutritional foods they should be eating—fruits, vegetables, whole grains, lean meats, and fish. Their bodies not only cannot keep up, they are actually breaking down.

But what are the short-term effects of excessive consumption of carbonated beverages? What happens right away when someone drinks these sugary drinks?

Sugar and Caffeine Crashes

The quickest short-term effects from drinking too much soda are energy rushes followed by equally

A 12-ounce (340 g) bottle of soda can include as much as 13 tablespoons (192 ml) of sugar. How's that for sugar shock?

intense crashes. Because of all the sugar, caffeine, and calories contained in most carbonated beverages, there will be an initial jolt of energy delivered by the drink. But this will be short-lived.

Within just a few minutes, the person will begin feeling sluggish as his or her metabolism is forced to work harder to process the sudden excess of sugar. Poor sleep patterns are also an immediate side effect of drinking too many carbonated beverages. The ups and downs created by the caffeine and sugar keep the body from being able to rest properly. This leads to fatigue and a lack of mental sharpness and concentration, which can be dangerous and result in serious accidents. Also, sleep is necessary for the body to heal itself and regenerate new, healthy cells. Chronic sleep disturbance and deprivation can short-circuit this natural healing process.

Caffeine Withdrawal Symptoms

Many carbonated beverages, especially colas, contain caffeine. Caffeine is a stimulating drug that increases the heart rate and blood pressure. People who consume caffeinated soft drinks on a regular basis have reported mild withdrawal-like symptoms when they do not have the drink. Irritability, headaches, poor concentration, and fatigue or sleepiness are all symptoms of caffeine withdrawal. Caffeine is addictive, but the energy boost it provides diminishes the more one ingests it. So, in order to get that kick, one must drink more and more of a caffeinated beverage over time. If the caffeine comes in the form of soda, this means that the drinker is also ingesting more and more sugar (or artificial sweetener), artificial colors and flavors, and other chemicals.

What About Diet Drinks?

Most people think that diet sodas are a healthy alternative to high-sugar sodas. Unfortunately, this is just not the case. These diet drinks use artificial chemical sweeteners to keep their calorie counts down. The body is fooled by the sweeteners and thinks it is getting sugar. The body reacts metabolically, digesting and processing the sweetener as if it was real sugar. For this reason, diet soda drinkers may experience an initial and minor change in weight (due to the reduced calories of artificial sweeteners). However, diet soda drinkers will find that they are consuming even more chemical additives than are usually found in regular sodas, so there are no long-term "health" benefits to diet sodas at all.

Some of the most common diet soda additives have been tested on lab rats, and links were made to cancers and other serious health problems subsequently developed by the rats. After years of government debate, these same chemicals were later approved for use in diet soda. If someone must have a carbonated beverage, carbonated water or seltzer is the healthiest option. Chemical-filled diet sodas are simply not the answer.

The cycle of highs and crashes associated with sugary and caffeinated beverages is exhausting and strongly affects one's mood and productivity. Swinging between high energy and sluggishness, perkiness and grumpiness, is not a very pleasant or efficient way to go about one's day. Water and milk are much better alternatives. Water keeps the body hydrated and flushed of toxins, resulting in higher sustained energy levels. Milk helps build bones, provides steady levels of energy, and creates a feeling of fullness. This prevents snacking and binge eating. Carbonated beverages should only be consumed rarely and on special occasions. Even then one should be sure to carefully note the actual serving size (remember, a single bottle may actually contain two-and-a-half servings) and not overdo it.

Depression

What other effects can sodas have on the people who drink them? Some studies have suggested a link between sugary foods and drinks and depression. When the diets of people suffering from depression were examined in an international study, it was found that depressed people consumed a lot more sugar than did the general population. It was also found that when these people cut their sugar and caffeine intake—two of the most important components of carbonated beverages—their moods improved. When they started to consume sugar and caffeine again, however, their depression often returned.

The consumption of sugary sodas is linked to the obesity epidemic in North America, as well as a host of other diseases.

Want to see your teeth rot away? Keep pounding down those sugary beverages! In this person's mouth, acid has eroded the enamel of the teeth.

Tooth Decay and Weakening Bones

There are other short-term effects associated with consuming sugary carbonated beverages. Tooth decay is a result of too much sugar. Sugars from the beverages can linger in the mouth and mix with acids in the saliva. Over time, this sugary acid can wear down the enamel on teeth and cause cavities. Untreated cavities can lead to tooth rot, dangerous infections, and bad breath. Tooth decay can happen rather quickly. Teeth can rot in a matter of weeks or months if a person does not care for his or her teeth properly and continues to drink carbonated beverages and consume other sugary snack foods regularly.

Tooth decay and gum disease can also result from not consuming enough milk and calcium, which bones and teeth require to stay healthy and strong. In fact, in addition to tooth problems, doctors have begun to see an increase in broken bones in children under the age of eighteen. Since 1970, there has been an increase of more than 50 percent in cases of broken bones in boys and 30 percent in girls. Many doctors and nutritionists have attributed this increase to a reduction in milk consumption by children and resulting calcium deficiencies.

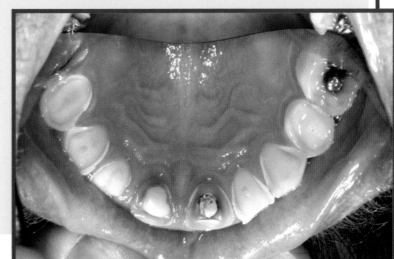

In addition, the bones and joints of increasingly obese children with calcium-poor diets are being placed under so much stress that they are requiring hip and joint surgery.

As many North American families have increasingly replaced milk with carbonated beverages, growing kids who need calcium from milk are not getting it. In the middle of the twentieth century, milk was consumed four times as much as soda. Current statistics show that this trend has been reversed as soda has replaced milk as the beverage of choice throughout the day. Indeed, soft drinks are a $68 billion-a-year business in the United States and account for about 10 percent of the calories Americans consume.

Milk is also an important source of vitamins D, A, and B12, essential nutrients that carbonated beverages do not provide. Many companies that make carbonated beverages are now trying to add nutrients to soda. But these added nutrients are not metabolized by our bodies as well or as efficiently as those coming from other drinks that contain these nutrients naturally, such as all-natural fresh fruit and vegetable juices.

3 --- THE LONG-TERM EFFECTS

Not many children or teens worry too much about what their health will be like as adults. Yet, thanks to the unhealthy North American diet, the future is now. Doctors are now seeing children younger than ten years old with diseases usually seen in people approaching sixty! Imagine the long-term effects a poor diet might have on a child who develops diabetes or heart disease at the age of ten. Imagine dying at the age of forty after already suffering decades of illness in youth, instead of living a healthy life for as many as eighty or ninety more or less trouble-free years. Overconsumption of carbonated beverages is a major culprit in the early onset of disease.

Diabetes

Diabetes is a disease in which the sufferer has high blood sugar (glucose) levels because the body either doesn't produce enough insulin or the body's cells don't respond to the insulin that is

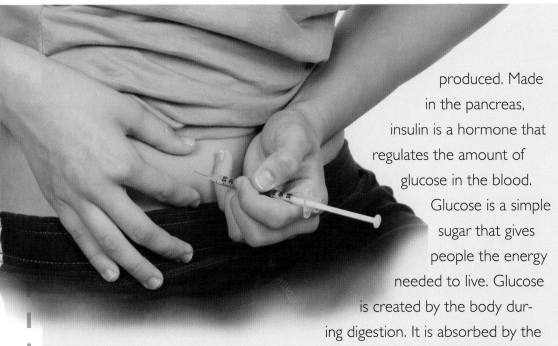

produced. Made in the pancreas, insulin is a hormone that regulates the amount of glucose in the blood. Glucose is a simple sugar that gives people the energy needed to live. Glucose is created by the body during digestion. It is absorbed by the body's cells and provides them with the energy needed to function properly.

Type 1 diabetes is also known as juvenile diabetes because it often afflicts children (though adults can develop it, too). It is caused by an immune system problem that results in the body's failure to produce insulin. Type 1 diabetics must inject themselves with insulin to maintain proper levels of the hormone and lower their blood sugar levels.

Type 2 diabetes used to mainly afflict adults because its onset is more closely related to poor dietary and lifestyle habits. With type 2 diabetes, the body's cells become insulin resistant. They therefore do not absorb glucose effectively, leading to high levels of glucose (high blood sugar levels) in the bloodstream. Type 2 diabetes is common among people who don't exercise, are overweight, smoke,

Injecting the body with insulin is an everyday event for diabetics. Without the insulin, their bodies could go into shock.

and have a high-fat diet. Conversely, people who exercise regularly, have a healthy and low-fat diet, don't smoke, drink little or no alcohol, and maintain a normal weight can reduce their chances of developing type 2 diabetes by almost 90 percent.

Drinking sweetened carbonated beverages is an important piece of the diabetes puzzle. Drinking sugary drinks too frequently will keep the pancreas working too hard for too long because it is constantly trying to regulate overly high glucose levels. Over time, the body will become resistant to all the excess insulin being produced to control the high glucose levels. Once the body's cells become insulin resistant, blood sugar levels shoot up. Eventually, the pancreas wears out and cannot keep up. When this happens to a person and his or her body cannot produce or absorb enough insulin to regulate the glucose, diabetes has taken hold. And the consequences can be severe—vision loss, nerve damage, cardiovascular disease, kidney disease and failure, coma, and even death.

For example, excess sugar in a diabetic's limbs damages the nerves and can result in numbness. The person can also bruise very easily. A diabetic's extremities (lower legs and arms) are unable to get fuel due to insulin resistance. The result is a decrease of muscle and an increase in fat. Reduced blood flow to a diabetic's extremities can greatly increase the risk of infection. Some infections become so serious that affected limbs may have to be amputated. A diabetic's eyes can also be affected, resulting in blurred or double vision.

If diabetes is left uncontrolled, it can lead to high blood pressure, heart attack, and stroke. Many people with type 2 diabetes are obese. Higher levels of cholesterol are produced when a person is obese, and this increased fat in

A healthy liver should appear smooth. This one shows symptoms of a disease called cirrhosis, which can be caused by a preservative in sodas.

the blood eventually clogs arteries. In addition, an insulin-resistant person's body will produce too much insulin to compensate for the cells' resistance to the hormone. This excess insulin causes the liver to produce excess fatty acids, leading to liver disease. Strokes are related to both high blood pressure and diabetes. A stroke occurs when a blood clot blocks an artery carrying blood to the brain. Diabetes, high blood pressure, and being overweight can all lead to stroke and heart disease over time.

There are early warning signs that diabetes is developing. These include extreme thirst, frequent urination, sudden changes to vision, an increased appetite, sudden weight loss, and unusual drowsiness. Anyone experiencing one or more of these symptoms should see a doctor immediately.

Cirrhosis

Cirrhosis is a chronic (ongoing and long-term) form of liver disease. It is often found in people with alcoholism or hepatitis (inflammation of the liver). Yet researchers have found that some cases of cirrhosis are also caused by a preservative in sodas called sodium benzoate (sometimes also known as E211).

The chemical is made from benzoic acid, which can be found in small amounts in nature. For example, it is found in some kinds of berries. However, sodium benzoate is chemically produced in large quantities and put into sodas to prevent mold from forming in the can or bottle.

Sodium benzoate has been used for decades, but its long-term effects have taken a very long time to show up in humans. In addition to cirrhosis, scientists also fear that sodium benzoate may cause cancer when consumed over a long period of time. This is because when the preservative is mixed with vitamin C, which is found in many soft drinks, a carcinogenic (toxic) substance called benzene is produced.

Cirrhosis can result in bad breath, fluid retention, painful bone inflammation, deformity of the fingers, growth of male breast tissue, shrinking of the testicles, impotence, infertility, shrinking or swelling of the liver, yellowing of the skin and eyes, coma, and death.

Parkinson's Disease

Parkinson's disease is a progressive disorder of the nervous system. It causes tremors in the patient, as well as stiff and slow muscular movements that are difficult to control. Some scientists have linked this disease to the same preservative in sodas that causes cirrhosis—sodium benzoate.

People Power!

When people choose not to buy a food or drink that is unhealthy, the company that produces it definitely takes notice. When its sales begin to slump, the company will do anything it can to lure consumers back by giving them what they want. Beverage companies have been hearing the complaints of consumers who do not like what they are seeing on the store shelves. For example, it is now easier to find sodas in smaller serving sizes that total about one hundred calories. More sodas are now available that contain no artificial ingredients, including artificial sweeteners, colors, and flavors. These increased choices make it easier for consumers to take charge of their own health. When consumers vote with their wallet at the supermarket by avoiding unwholesome drinks and snacks and buying healthier alternatives, they are leading a dietary revolution and helping forge a healthier world.

The soda preservative is thought to attack DNA and damages the mitochondria. Mitochondria are subunits in cells that act as a sort of power plant for the cells. They also control cell cycles, cell growth, and cell death. When attacked by sodium benzoate, the DNA sometimes completely shuts down. Parkinson's is normally associated with middle-aged and elderly people, but scientists are now finding this disease in younger people. This is perhaps due in part to soda consumption and the presence of sodium benzoate.

Heart Disease

Diabetes and obesity put people at an increased risk for developing heart disease. But a 2007 study from the Boston University School of Medicine made a much more direct link between soda drinking and heart disease. The study found that people who drank soda (including diet soda) every day—even just one drink—were at a much higher risk of developing metabolic syndrome. This is a common cause of heart disease. Metabolic syndrome is a disease that often occurs in people who are overweight (especially if the weight accumulates at the waistline), have high blood pressure, have high blood sugar even when they are fasting, and have high cholesterol.

Cancer

What if someone drinks soda only twice a week, maybe on the weekends? Surprisingly, the long-term health risks for the moderate soda drinker are not much better than for the regular soda drinker. A recent study from the University of Minnesota has found that people who drink as few as two sodas per week are twice as likely to

These are pancreatic cancer cells as seen under a microscope.

develop pancreatic cancer than are people who do not. The studies tested only regular sodas, not diet sodas.

The pancreas is the place where insulin is produced in an effort to balance and regulate the body's blood sugar level. The more sugary drinks a person consumes, the more insulin his or her body will produce in an attempt to control the overabundant glucose. The pancreas will be working overtime. This may cause an abnormal growth of pancreatic cells, which results in cancer.

Acid Reflux

After just a few sips of a carbonated beverage, drinkers soon experience a familiar side effect: burping and belching. Over time, however, far more serious problems can develop. Regularly drinking large amounts of carbonated beverages can cause an upset stomach and bloating. Some people who are overweight or who have sensitive stomachs can get heartburn or acid reflux from soda consumption.

Acid reflux is the term for what occurs when gastric acid is regurgitated (sent back up) from the stomach to the esophagus. The esophagus contains a sphincter (a sort of muscular flap) that closes the stomach shut so that food will stay within it. Yet the sphincter opens to allow carbon dioxide from the stomach to be released. When someone experiences acid reflux, this flap remains open and stomach acids back up and burn the esophagus or throat. Medication and even surgery are needed to correct the problem.

People with acid reflex become far more likely to develop esophageal cancer due to the damage to the esophagus wreaked by the acid. This is a very serious cancer. It is often diagnosed late, and only 5 percent of esophageal cancer patients remain alive five years after diagnosis.

> When acids wear away the lining of the stomach, a hole like this can result. It's called an ulcer.

Ulcers

The stomach is lined with a protective coating that keeps digestive acids from digesting the stomach itself. Carbonated beverages are very bubbly and acidic. When too much of this abrasive acid is deposited in the stomach on a consistent basis, it can wear away the protective lining in some spots, and small burns and holes can occur. These are called ulcers, and they can form in the stomach and small intestine.

In addition to tears and holes, ulcers can cause great pain. They can also result in hemorrhages (heavy bleeding due to erosion of a blood vessel in the stomach or intestine), vomiting, and blood in the stool (solid waste). Some ulcers even become cancerous. If no dietary changes are made and bleeding ulcers are left untreated, surgery may eventually be required to stop the bleeding and repair the damage.

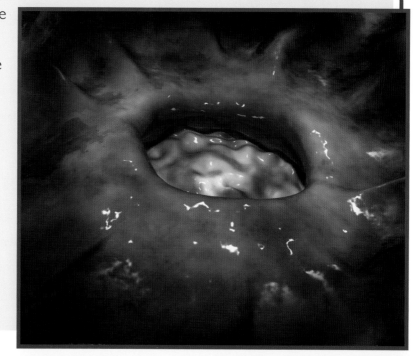

GET HEALTHY NOW!

Obesity has become such a major and widespread problem in the United States that it costs as much as $147 billion a year in medical expenses. All of the medical ailments related to excessive drinking of carbonated beverages and other poor dietary choices that have been discussed in this book are expensive to diagnose and treat. Many of these illnesses and diseases have no cure, and the patient must live with permanent damage to his or her body. Increasingly, many doctors, nutritionists, politicians, insurers, and ordinary people believe that by changing the diet of North Americans, society will not only save lots of money, but also save millions of lives.

Soda Soda Everywhere!

How can people change their diets and improve their dietary choices? Are they expected to give up carbonated beverages entirely? Back in the days

when most people did not live minutes away from twenty-four-hour convenience stores or pass vending machines in nearly every public building, a soda was thought of as a sweet—and infrequent—treat. Having a cola, root beer, or grape soda was a special occasion.

Today, sodas are so readily available that they are often thought of as an essential part of every meal and snack. People should return to the idea that carbonated beverages must only be consumed on special occasions—like parties,

You don't have to look very hard to find soda machines in public buildings, including schools and hospitals.

cookouts, and other infrequent celebrations. If they do this, they could greatly decrease their daily intake of countless grams of sugar and chemically processed preservatives.

Making Better Choices

Cutting down on soda may be easier said than done, however. What can a person do who is at school, in a convenience store, or at a party and wants to choose something tasty to drink? When choosing a beverage, remember that milk is by far the most nutritious beverage. It provides calcium that the body needs to grow and stay strong, it is loaded with vitamins A and D, and it helps create a full feeling that prevents overeating or snacking between meals.

Water is also always an excellent beverage choice. Water is needed by the human body to maintain all of its functions, and it helps metabolize food. It's just about the best thing a person can put into his or her body. Best of all, it has no added sugar, salt, or artificial chemical coloring, flavoring, or sweeteners. When a little extra flavor kick is desired, a wedge of lemon, lime, or orange can be squeezed and dropped into a glass of water.

Some people miss the carbonation of sodas when they try to go without it. In these cases, one should consider seltzer or mineral waters. These are basically ordinary water to which carbon dioxide has been added for extra fizz. Check the nutrition and ingredient labels on these beverages, however. Make sure they do not include too many extra calories, added sugar or artificial sweeteners, or too much sodium.

Water refreshes and rehydrates the body and has no additives. It's a great alternative to soda, especially during and after exercise and sporting events.

Fruit juices are also a healthier alternative to sodas, but not all fruit juices are created equal. Many have a lot of added sugar and even artificial colors and flavors. Some do not even include real fruit. Even fruit juices made with natural fruits can have added sugars and high fructose corn syrup. Fresh-squeezed juices with nothing added to the fruit are always the best choice. Consider making juices at home, with a blender or juicer. This way, you can control what goes into the drink and you can come up with interesting and delicious fruit combinations.

When choosing beverages, be sure to study and compare the drinks' ingredient lists and nutrition labels. When comparing one brand or type of beverage to another, the healthy choice usually becomes clear quite quickly. Typically, the healthier choices have fewer ingredients, less sugar, less sodium, no artificial colors, flavors, or sweeteners, no high fructose corn syrup, no caffeine, and fewer calories. A long ingredient list of chemical additives that are difficult to pronounce is a sure sign that a beverage is not the healthiest choice. Remember that you are in control of what you drink. And don't forget to look at the serving sizes on the labels. One small beverage bottle usually contains a lot more than one serving.

Frozen drinks and packaged and processed fruit juices are often loaded with sugars. It's always best to choose water or fresh-squeezed fruit juices.

The cool, fizzy sweetness of soda and cola may be a refreshing taste sensation, but that is not nearly enough to make them a worthwhile beverage. The list of negative side effects and serious diseases that regular soda consumption can lead to is long and incredibly disgusting. Everything from bad breath, tooth decay, and the jitters to life-threatening illnesses like diabetes, heart disease, and cancer can result from daily soda drinking. Given this sobering information, the choice of what to drink becomes far simpler. Except on rare and special occasions, we should choose to drink cool, clear water. By choosing water and other healthy beverage alternatives, we are also choosing a lifetime of good health.

TEN GREAT QUESTIONS TO ASK A NUTRITIONIST

1: How much weight will I lose if I stop drinking soda?

2: How can I help get soda vending machines out of my school?

3: Are seltzers and mineral waters bad for my health, even if they don't have added sugar or sweeteners?

4: How can I tell how many servings are in a fountain drink ordered in a restaurant?

5: Is there any nutritional value at all in a glass of soda?

6: Are there any brands of soda that are healthier than others?

7: Should I avoid all foods with high fructose corn syrup and other sugar substitutes?

8: Is a beverage better for me if it is made with real sugar, rather than with sugar substitutes?

9: What can I do if I am at a party that serves only sodas?

10: Diabetes runs in my family. How can I change my diet to help avoid developing it myself?

GLOSSARY

acid reflux A condition that causes the regurgitation of stomach acids into the esophagus.

caffeine A stimulant drug that naturally occurs in the beans, leaves, and fruits of some plants and is found in coffee, tea, energy drinks, and many colas and other soft drinks.

cancer A disease caused by abnormal cell division in a certain part of the body.

carbonation The result of the dissolving of carbon dioxide in a liquid; creates the bubbly, fizzy quality of sodas.

cirrhosis A chronic and potentially fatal liver disorder caused by the replacement of healthy liver cells with scarred, fibrous, and damaged tissue.

diabetes A disease in which the pancreas does not produce any or enough insulin, or the body's cells cannot process the insulin that is produced.

esophagus The muscular tube through which food passes on its way to the stomach.

fatty acids Acids that are produced when fats are broken down. They can be used for energy by most types of cells and help move oxygen through the bloodstream to all parts of the body. They also aid cell membrane development, strength, and function and are essential to organ and tissue health.

gastric acid A secretion produced in the stomach that aids digestion and the breaking down of proteins.

glucose A simple sugar that is needed for energy in living things; it powers the cell's activities.

hemorrhage Heavy bleeding due to erosion of a blood vessel in the stomach or intestine.

hepatitis Inflammation of the liver.

high fructose corn syrup An artificial sweetener found in processed foods; used in place of sugar.

insulin A hormone made by the pancreas that regulates glucose levels in the blood.

Parkinson's disease A progressive disease of the nervous system that causes muscular tension and tremors.

stroke An interruption in the blood flow to the brain caused by a burst or blocked blood vessel; sometimes referred to as a brain attack.

ulcer In the case of a peptic, or stomach, ulcer, an erosion of the protective mucous membrane that lines the stomach or the first part of the small intestine.

FOR MORE INFORMATION

Centers for Disease Control and Prevention (CDC)

1600 Clifton Road

Atlanta, GA 30333

(800) CDC-INFO [232-4636]

Web site: http://www.cdc.gov

The CDC's mission is to collaborate to create the expertise, information, and tools that people and communities need to protect their health through health promotion, prevention of disease, injury and disability, and preparedness for new health threats.

Children's Health Foundation

400 West Main Street, Suite 210

Aspen, CO 81611

(888) 920-4750

Web site: http://www.childrenshealthfoundation.net

The Children's Health Foundation is a nonprofit organization dedicated to making changes in schools and communities that promote health, including the prevention of childhood obesity.

Diabetic Children's Foundation

785 Plymouth, Suite 210

Mont Royal, QC H4P 1B3

Canada

(800) 731-9683

Web site: http://diabetes-children.ca

The Diabetic Children's Foundation promotes the health of Canadian children and teens who are living with diabetes. The foundation also has a summer camp for its members.

Health Canada

Address Locator 0900C2

Ottawa, ON KIA 0K9

Canada

(866) 225-0709

Web site: http://www.hc-sc.gc.ca/index-eng.php

Health Canada is the federal department responsible for helping Canadians maintain and improve their health. Its goal is for Canada to be among the countries with the healthiest people in the world. To achieve this goal, Health Canada relies on high-quality scientific research as the basis for its work. It conducts ongoing consultations with Canadians to determine how to best meet their long-term health care needs. Health Canada communicates information about disease prevention to protect Canadians from avoidable risks. And it encourages Canadians to take an active role in their health, such as increasing their level of physical activity and eating well.

International Food Information Council Foundation

1100 Connecticut Avenue, NW, Suite 430

Washington, DC 20036

(202) 296-6540

Web site: http://www.foodinsight.org

The International Food Information Council Foundation is an independent, nonprofit organization dedicated to public education about food, nutrition, and food safety.

National Institutes of Health (NIH)

9000 Rockville Pike

Bethesda, MD 20892

(301) 496-4000

Web site: http://www.nih.gov/index.html

The NIH's mission is to seek fundamental knowledge about the nature and behavior of living systems and the application of that knowledge to enhance health, lengthen life, and reduce the burdens of illness and disability.

School Nutrition Association

120 Waterfront Street, Suite 300

National Harbor, MD 20745

(301) 686-3100

Web site: http://www.schoolnutrition.org

The School Nutrition Association provides education and training to those interested in advancing the nutrition of school lunches and providing nutritious meals to children.

Shaping America's Youth

120 NW 9th Avenue, Suite 216

Portland, OR 97209-3326

(800) SAY-9221 [729-9221]

Web site: http://www.shapingamericasyouth.org

Shaping America's Youth provides information about community programs across the United States that attempt to increase physical activity and improve nutrition among American children.

Web Sites

Due to the changing nature of Internet links, Rosen Publishing has developed an online list of Web sites related to the subject of this book. This site is updated regularly. Please use this link to access the list:

http://www.rosenlinks.com/idf/bev

FOR FURTHER READING

Bennett, Andrea T., and James H. Kessler. *Sunlight, Skyscrapers, and Soda-Pop: The Wherever-You-Look Science Book*. Washington, DC: American Chemical Society, 2003.

Briggs, Margaret. *Bicarbonate of Soda: A Very Versatile Natural Substance*. Edinburgh, Scotland: Black & White Publishing, 2007.

Cunningham, Kevin. *Colas* (Global Products). Ann Arbor, MI: Cherry Lake Publishing, 2007.

Grunes, Barbara. *Diabetes Snacks, Treats, & Easy Eats for Kids: 130 Recipes for the Foods Kids Really Like to Eat*. Chicago, IL: Surrey Books, 2006.

Platt, Richard. *They Ate What?!: The Weird History of Food*. Minneapolis, MN: T&N Children's Publishing, 2006.

Pollan, Michael. *The Omnivore's Dilemma for Kids: The Secrets Behind What You Eat* (Young Readers Edition). New York, NY: Dial, 2009.

Schlosser, Eric, and Charles Wilson. *Chew on This: Everything You Don't Want to Know About Fast Food*. New York, NY: Sandpiper, 2007.

Schuh, Mari C., and Barbara J. Rolls. *Healthy Snacks*. Mankato, MN: Coughlan Publishing, 2006.

Spurlock, Morgan. *Don't Eat This Book: Fast Food and the Supersizing of America*. New York, NY: Berkeley Trade, 2006.

Zinczenko, David, and Matt Goulding. *Eat This, Not That!* New York, NY: Rodale Press, 2008.

BIBLIOGRAPHY

Appleton, Nancy, and G. N. Jacobs. *Suicide by Sugar: A Startling Look at Our #1 National Addiction.* Garden City Park, NY: Square One Publishers, 2009.

Bakalar, Nicholas. "Fructose-Sweetened Beverages Linked to Heart Risks." *New York Times*, April 23, 2009. Retrieved December 2009 (http://www.nytimes.com/2009/04/23/health/23sugar.html?scp=1&sq=Fructose-Sweetened%20Beverages%20Linked%20to%20Heart%20Risks&st=cse).

Bellis, Mary. "Introduction to Pop: The History of Soft Drinks: Soft Drinks Can Trace Their History Back to the Mineral Water Found in Springs." About.com. Retrieved March 2010 (http://inventors.about.com/od/foodrelatedinventions/a/soft_drinks.htm).

Bellis, Mary. "Introduction to Pop: The History of Soft Drinks Timeline." About.com. Retrieved March 2010 (http://inventors.about.com/od/sstartinventions/a/soft_drink.htm).

CBSNews.com. "Study: Soda Linked to Pancreatic Cancer." February 9, 2010. Retrieved March 2010 (http://www.cbsnews.com/stories/2010/02/09/health/main6189455.shtml).

Centers for Disease Control and Prevention. "Study Estimates Medical Cost of Obesity May Be as High as $147 Billion Annually." July 27, 2009. Retrieved March 2010 (http://www.cdc.gov/media/pressrel/2009/r090727.htm).

Critser, Greg. *Fat Land: How Americans Became the Fattest People in the World.* New York, NY: Houghton Mifflin Company, 2003.

Doheny, Kathleen. "One Daily Soda May Boost Heart Disease." WebMD.com, July 23, 2007. Retrieved March 2010 (http://www.webmd.com/heart/metabolic-syndrome/news/20070723/1-daily-soda-may-boost-heart-disease).

Johnson, Richard J., and Timothy Gower. *The Sugar Fix: The High-Fructose Fallout That Is Making You Fat and Sick*. New York, NY: Pocket, 2009.

Juvenile Diabetes Research Foundation International. "What Is Diabetes?" March 2010 (http://www.jdrf.org/index.cfm?fuseaction=home.viewPage&page_id=71927021-99EA-4D04-92E8463E607C84E1).

Medina, Jennifer. "In Schools, New Rules on Snacks for Sale." *New York Times*, October 7, 2009. Retrieved December 2009 (http://www.nytimes.com/2009/10/07/nyregion/07contract.html?_r=1&scp=1&sq=jennifer%20medina%20snacks&st=cse).

Okie, Susan. *Fed Up!: Winning the War Against Childhood Obesity*. Washington, DC: Joseph Henry Press, 2005.

Poirot, Carolyn. "High-Fructose Corn Syrup Fueling Obesity Epidemic, Doctors Say." *Seattle Times*, December 4, 2005. Retrieved December 2009 (http://seattletimes.nwsource.com/html/health/2002658491_healthsyrup04.html).

PR Newswire. "Kids Breaking More Bones: Doctors Say Soft Drinks Poor Substitute for Milk." TheFreeLibrary.com, March 23, 2004. Retrieved December 2009 (http://www.thefreelibrary.com/Kids+Breaking+More+Bones%3B+-+Doctors+Say+Soft+Drinks+Poor+Substitute...-a0114523014).

Schimelpfening, Nancy. "Drop the Soda Habit and Feel Better." About.com, October 7, 2009. Retrieved March 2010 (http://depression.about.com/b/2009/10/07/drop-the-soda-habit-and-feel-better.htm).

Schlosser, Eric. *Fast Food Nation*. New York, NY: Harper Perennial, 2002.

Skopitz, Kimberly. "History of Soft Drinks." Essortment.com, 2002. Retrieved March 2010 (http://www.essortment.com/all/historyofsoft_rntg.htm essortment.com).

Tartamella Lisa, Elaine Herscher, and Chris Woolston. *Generation Extra Large: Rescuing Our Children from the Epidemic of Obesity*. New York, NY: Basic Books, 2006.

Valentine, Judith. "Soft Drinks: America's Other Drinking Problem." Weston A. Price Foundation, May 26, 2002. Retrieved March 2010 (http://www.westonaprice.org/Soft-Drinks-America-s-Other-Drinking-Problem.html).

White, Mike. "Some Scientists Believe Soda Pop May Cause Cirrhosis of the Liver and Parkinson's." AssociatedContent.com, June 1, 2007. Retrieved March 2010 (http://www.associatedcontent.com/article/261745/some_scientists_believe_soda_pop_may.html?cat=51).

INDEX

About the Author

Adam Furgang is a writer who has written several books on science, health, and nutrition topics, including *Salty and Sugary Snacks: The Incredibly Disgusting Story*. He lives in upstate New York with his wife and two children.

Photo Credits

Cover, pp. 1, 4–5, 6, 14, 15, 21, 30 Shutterstock.com; p. 7 Petretti's Coca-Cola Collectibles Price Guide, 12th edition (Krause Publications); p. 8 Tim Boyle/Getty Images; pp. 10–11 © www.istockphoto.com/Joselito Briones; p. 18 Digital Vision/Getty Images; p. 19 © Edward H. Gill/Custom Medical Stock Photo; p. 22 Hemera/Thinkstock; pp. 24–25 © Custom Medical Stock Photo; p. 27 Anne Weston/Electron Microscopy Unit, Cancer Research UK/Visuals Unlimited, Inc./Getty Images; p. 29 3D Clinic/Getty Images; p. 31 George Ruhe/Bloomberg via Getty Images; p. 33 Digital Vision/Thinkstock; p. 34 © www.istockphoto.com/4x6.

Designer: Les Kanturek; Photo Researcher: Amy Feinberg